NEW YORK

VICKY SHIPTON

Level 3

Series Editors: Andy Hopkins and Jocelyn Potter

Pearson Education Limited
Edinburgh Gate, Harlow,
Essex CM20 2JE, England
and Associated Companies throughout the world.

ISBN: 978-1-4058-8197-5

First published by Penguin Books 2003
This edition first published 2008

3 5 7 9 10 8 6 4

Text copyright © Vicky Shipton 2003
Maps by Alan Fraser, Pennant Inc.

Design by John Fordham
Colour reproduction by Spectrum Colour, Ipswich

Typeset by Graphicraft Ltd, Hong Kong
Set in 9.5/14pt The Serif Light
Printed in China
SWTC/03

For a complete list of the titles available in the Penguin Readers series please write to your local
Pearson Longman office or to: Penguin Readers Marketing Department, Pearson Education,
Edinburgh Gate, Harlow, Essex CM20 2JE, England.

Contents

Introduction

You can see who the visitors are in New York. They walk around looking up all the time! New York is famous for its skyscrapers. There are many different styles of building. Some are beautiful, some are not. Together they are one of the most wonderful sights in the world.

Tourists can buy T-shirts that say "I Love New York." This is true for New Yorkers. They are very proud of their city, sometimes calling it "the world's city" or "the capital of the world." There are many wonderful things to do there. You can eat food from all around the world. You can shop all day. You can spend time in a big, beautiful park and never leave the city.

But New York is not without problems, too.

In this book you can read the story of the greatest city in the United States.

Vicky Shipton is from Michigan, in the United States. She lived in Turkey and England for a long time before returning to the U.S. Now she lives in Cambridge, England, with her husband and two daughters.

She loves to visit New York. She once drove for 16 hours to reach the city. "But I wasn't tired," says Vicky. "You cannot feel tired in New York!"

The "Big Apple"

New York is possibly the most famous city in the world. Every year, millions of tourists come to see its skyscrapers and busy streets. There is no other place in the world like it. To New Yorkers, it is THE city—the most exciting in the world. The city that never sleeps.

What's in a Name?

Many people call New York the "Big Apple" or just "the Apple." No one is really sure where this name comes from. Some people think that jazz musicians first used it in the 1920s. They meant the place where everything happened.

New York City is on the east coast of the United States, in the state of New York. It is the biggest city in the state—in fact, with over 8 million people it is the biggest city in the United States—but it is not the state capital. That is Albany, 156 miles (231 kilometers) north of New York.

The city and the rest of the state are like two different worlds. The state has green hills, farms, and mountains. More than half of the state is forest. New York State is the largest on the east coast, but fewer than 11 million people live there outside of the city.

If you are planning to visit New York, remember to check the weather. In the winter, it has lots of snow and is very cold. Almost 100 inches (254 centimeters) of snow fall every year. But in the summer, it is very hot. It can reach almost 100°F (36°C).

The Five Parts of New York

When people think of New York, they usually think of Manhattan. Manhattan is an island just 13.3 miles (21.5 kilometers) long and 2.3 miles (3.7 kilometers) wide. But Manhattan is not all of New York. It is only one of five areas known as "boroughs." They are Manhattan, Queens, the Bronx, Brooklyn, and Staten Island.

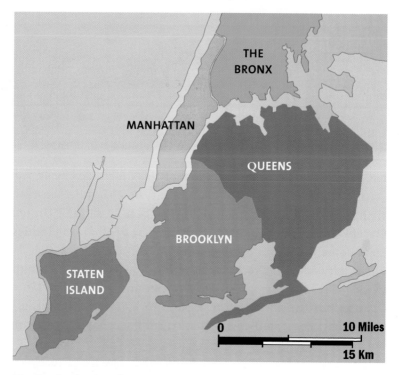

The five boroughs of New York

Manhattan

Manhattan is the place where you can see most of the city's famous buildings and sights. It has the Hudson River on the west, and the East River and the Harlem River on the east.

Queens

Queens is the largest area. The bridge from Manhattan to Queens goes across Roosevelt Island, a smaller island.

The Bronx

For a long time, many people did not want to visit the Bronx because they were afraid of crime. In the last few years, there has been less crime in this area.

Staten Island

Visitors to Staten Island are often surprised to find lakes and green hills. There are many small houses with front- and back-yards.

Brooklyn

Only three US cities—Los Angeles, Chicago, and Houston—have larger populations than Brooklyn.

There are three big airports close to the city. Newark Airport is in New Jersey. John F. Kennedy (JFK) and La Guardia airports are both in Queens.

There is more than one way to reach Manhattan. You can cross one of the many bridges. You can drive under the river. Or you can cross the water on a ferry.

The City and the Island

New Yorkers call Manhattan "the City." When they say "the Island," they mean Long Island, the island to the east of New York. Some New Yorkers like to leave "the City" during the summer and play on "the Island."

The City in the Sky

You can see who the visitors are in New York. They walk around looking up all the time! New York is famous for its skyscrapers. There are many different styles of building. Some are beautiful, some are not. Together they are one of the most wonderful sights in the world.

The first skyscraper was built around 100 years ago. Before that, tall buildings were not possible. Each year brought different styles of building. There were two main reasons for each new style—builders' skills and city rules. The earlier buildings had to be smaller at the top than at the bottom. Later builders could make buildings that went straight up like big boxes. But in the last few years, New York City has introduced new rules. People do not want the streets below to be too dark in the shadow of big buildings.

New York was the perfect place for skyscrapers. On a small, crowded island, there was only one place to go—up. But this was not the only reason. New York was full of people with big dreams. The city's great buildings, reaching for the sky, were like a mirror to these big dreams.

Most of the city's skyscrapers are in the central area of Manhattan, known as "midtown." There is another group of skyscrapers in the financial area to the south.

Some of the city's most famous buildings are:

The Empire State Building

The builder of the Empire State Building, William F. Lamb, was asked to make it big. He did, finishing the world-famous building in 1931. It has 103 floors and is 1,454 feet (443 meters)

high. It was the tallest building in the world until 1970. The building fills one complete city block. Tourists can enjoy the views of the city from the 86th and the 102nd floors. On a clear day, you can see almost 80 miles (130 kilometers) from the 102nd floor!

The Empire State Building has been in many movies over the years. For example, Tom Hanks and Meg Ryan meet at the top of the building in *Sleepless in Seattle*. But the building's most famous movie is *King Kong* (1933, 2005). At the end, King Kong climbs to the top of the building. He fights off airplanes.

The Flatiron Building

When the city's first skyscraper, the Flatiron Building, was built in 1902, many people called it a big mistake. "It is ugly!" they said. "It will fall down!" "It looks like the front of a ship!" But now the Flatiron Building, with its unusual shape, is one of the favorite sights in the city.

The Chrysler Building was built to look like a car wheel

The Chrysler Building

For many people, the Chrysler Building is the most beautiful in the city. It was built between 1928 and 1930 by the car company Chrysler. It was the tallest building in the world . . . but only for a year. Then the Empire State Building was finished. The Chrysler Building was built to look like a car wheel. When it was finished, the first floor was a car showroom!

The World Trade Center

After 1973, two buildings in lower Manhattan looked down on the rest of the city—the two 110-floor towers of the World Trade Center. Around 50,000 people worked there. Tourists could view the city from the 107th floor of one of the towers.

On September 11, 2001, New York City changed forever when two airplanes were flown into the two towers of the World Trade Center. The buildings were completely destroyed and more than 3,000 people died. Many firefighters died, bravely trying to help the people in the buildings. The terrible pictures of that day were seen around the world.

Many people were grateful to Rudy Giuliani, New York's mayor at the time, in the difficult months that followed. The mayor was able to help the people of the city in their terrible sadness.

From March 11 until April 13, 2002, New Yorkers could look at two towers of light in the sky. They could remember the people who died on September 11.

Two towers of light in New York's night sky

A New City

The "New World"

Five hundred years ago, Algonquin Indians lived on and around Manhattan Island. The island was called "Manna Hatta"—"The Island of the Hills." The first European, Giovanni da Verrazano, was Italian. He arrived in 1524 hoping to become rich in the "New World." After he left, Europeans did not return to the area for many years.

New Amsterdam

In 1609, Henry Hudson came up the river to the island. (The Hudson River was later named after him.) Hudson was British, but he worked for a Dutch company. He was looking for a quick way to India! But Hudson understood immediately that the area was important. Other men arrived from Holland. They bought animal skins from the Indians for guns and cloth.

Then, in 1626, Peter Minuit, an employee of the Dutch West India Company, bought Manhattan Island from the Indians. He paid them with a few small gifts. The island cost him around $24! After that, the island was Dutch. The city was called New Amsterdam. By the 1640s, around 500 Europeans lived there.

A New Name

King Charles II of Britain wanted the island. On his orders, the British took the city in 1664. The city received a new name—New York. (York is a city in England.) Under British rule, the city's business grew. The population grew, too. By 1750, there were 16,000 people there.

France also wanted this area. The two countries fought the French and Indian War between 1754 and 1763. After the war, New York was still British … but not for long!

A New Country

The people of the city, like many other Americans, were becoming unhappy with Britain. They did not want to pay money to a government in Britain. They wanted to be free. In 1776, they started a war. The British soon took the city, but in the end they lost the war. In 1783, George Washington became president of the new country. His office was in Manhattan. But New York was only the capital of the new country for a year.

New Wars

Britain and America were at war again in 1812. The British stopped ships coming to Manhattan. The war ended in 1814. Less than fifty years later, there was another war. This was between states in the north and south of the country. Soldiers from New York fought on the side of the north.

A New Life

After 1800, more and more immigrants came to the United States from other countries. Many of them arrived in New York. Immigrants came from different countries at different times. In the 1830s there were large numbers of German immigrants. Soon more than 200,000 people lived in New York. Then, in the 1850s, a lot of Irish families moved to the city. In the 1880s and 1890s, people from Italy, Eastern Europe and Asia started to arrive. By 1898, there were more than 3 million people living in New York City. It was the largest city in the world at that time.

Why did so many people come to New York? A lot of them were running away from problems in their own countries. They could start a new life in the United States. They came to live the "American dream."

The Statue of Liberty

The Statue of Liberty is one of the most famous sights in the world. The statue was not made in the US. It was a gift from the people of France in 1884.

At first, the statue stood in Paris. It was brought to the US in pieces. But the city needed a lot of money to put the statue up on Bedloe's Island. For two years the statue stayed in 220 boxes!

The statue was the first sight of New York for many immigrants. The look in her eyes was a promise of a new start in a new world.

About the Lady

Here are some facts about the famous lady:

- The statue was by Frédéric-Auguste Bartholdi. He copied his mother's face!
- Gustave Eiffel helped to build the statue. He later built Paris's Eiffel Tower.
- The statue is 305 feet (93 meters) tall. There are 354 steps from the bottom of the statue to the crown.
- Visitors can look out from the bottom of the statue and from the crown. They cannot go up the arm to the statue's highest point.
- The seven points on the statue's crown are for the seven seas.
- There is a museum at the bottom of the statue.
- The name of Bedloe's Island was changed to Liberty Island.

Ellis Island

Before they could begin their new life, immigrants to New York had to stop on Ellis Island. Between 1892 and 1954, this place was the gateway to the US for almost 17 million new Americans.

Ellis Island did not just welcome new Americans. The officers there also decided who could not come into the US. New immigrants stood at last on American land. But the big question was this: Could they stay?

Most people took between two and five hours to pass through Ellis Island. In the station's early years, immigrants had to complete these tests:

- First, they answered 29 questions. (How old were they? What job did they do in their old country? Were they married? Could they read?)

- Then immigrants were sent to the second floor of the building. *This* was the second test. Doctors watched people as they walked up the stairs. If they were not healthy, they had to have more tests. Very sick people were sent back home.

- Immigrants were then asked the same 29 questions again. Were their answers the same as the first time?

After this last test, immigrants were free to go into the country. Information was kept about everyone. Often immigrants changed their names, wanting to make them more "American." They could change money for US dollars. Then they could begin their new life. Some bought a train ticket all the way to California. Others decided to take the ferry and make New York their home. In this big, busy city they could find jobs. But life was not always easy. Many people in the city were very poor. Many immigrants could only live in cheap, dark, dirty buildings. These "tenements" were too hot in the summer and too cold in the winter.

Money Talks

Ellis Island was not always fair in the early years. For some immigrants, their first day in the US taught them an important lesson ... about money.

- Most immigrants arrived by boat. On some boats first and second class passengers were checked and let into the city. The other passengers had to go to Ellis Island.
- Sometimes Ellis Island workers took money from immigrants.
- When immigrants bought American dollars, they did not always get a fair price.
- The trains sometimes had high prices for tickets only for people from Ellis Island.

But in 1901, President Theodore Roosevelt learned about the problems at Ellis Island. After that, things became better.

After Ellis Island closed, the buildings were empty for years. But in 1990, they were opened as a museum. Tourists can take the same ferry to Liberty Island and to Ellis Island. The museum at Ellis Island really tells the story of the people of the United States.

Many Americans come here, too. Often they want to learn more about their family history. More and more of Ellis Island's old information is on computer now. People can easily see how their relatives answered the questions. They can find out what their relatives brought with them for their new life in the US.

The People of New York

New York is still an international city. By 1990, one out of every three New Yorkers was born in another country. In the last few years, many immigrants have moved to New York from Asia and from South and Central America.

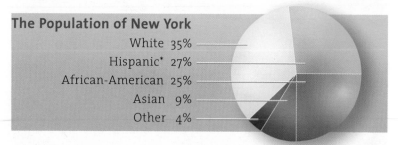

The Population of New York

White	35%
Hispanic*	27%
African-American	25%
Asian	9%
Other	4%

Each new wave of immigrants has changed and added to the feel of the city. At first, most people lived in neighborhoods with people from their own country. As time passed, more and more of them moved out. But the city still has neighborhoods that feel like a small part of the old country.

Here are some of the most famous neighborhoods in Manhattan:

Little Italy

There are more Italians in New York than in Rome! Italian immigrants started coming to New York around 1880. Little Italy became one of the first neighborhoods.

Now Little Italy is very small. Parts of it have become part of its bigger neighbor, Chinatown. But Little Italy is still a great place to visit. You can sometimes see a famous person like Al Pacino or Leonardo DiCaprio eating in one of the neighborhood's Italian restaurants.

* Hispanic: from countries where most people speak Spanish

A busy store in New York's Chinatown

Chinatown

More than 200,000 people live in Chinatown. Most of them are Asian, and around 150,000 are Chinese. This means that New York's Chinatown is the largest Chinese "city" outside Asia. The neighborhood has seven Chinese newspapers!

Chinatown was a small area of a few streets 100 years ago. Now it is over 4 square miles (10 square kilometers) and it is still growing. Millions of tourists come to enjoy the neighborhood's shops, great restaurants, and busy street life. Chinese New Year in January or February is always popular with tourists.

The Lower East Side

This area was the "gate to New York" for many immigrants. Most of the city's worst buildings were here. The area is still poor. It was home to many Jewish immigrants from Eastern Europe. Now the largest groups of immigrants to this area are from Puerto Rico and China.

Greenwich Village, SoHo, and TriBeCa

In most other parts of New York the streets are straight. This is not true in Greenwich Village. Many famous artists and writers lived in the neighborhood's old houses. Parts of the area have become quite expensive, but it is still a great place for artists, actors, and musicians. Many students live in Greenwich Village, too.

Both SoHo and TriBeCa are like Greenwich Village. SoHo got its name because it is **so**uth of **Ho**uston Street. Many artists moved to SoHo, but the price of apartments became very high.

The prices were better in TriBeCa, and in the last few years artists have moved there, too. Both SoHo and TriBeCa have small, interesting shops and restaurants.

All three areas have people from many different countries. But many people there have similar ideas and styles.

Harlem

Harlem is in the north of Manhattan, above Central Park. Around 100 years ago, African-Americans in the South of the United States started to move to cities in the North. Even more moved north after both world wars. In New York, many African-Americans went to Harlem.

Great African-American writers and musicians—Langston Hughes and Duke Ellington, for example—lived in Harlem. But after the late 1960s Harlem became quite dangerous, with a lot of crime and some race problems. Today Harlem is safer and people of all races have moved there. Bill Clinton now has an office in the area. A few local people did not want him there—they did not want the neighborhood to become too expensive! But most people were happy to have a famous neighbor.

El Barrio

El Barrio—"the neighborhood," in Spanish—is east of Harlem. The area is also known as Spanish Harlem. Puerto Ricans live in this part of Harlem, with Cubans and Dominicans.

People of different races and countries have not always mixed easily in New York. Even 100 years ago, there were sometimes big fights between gangs of people from different countries. In modern times, there are still problems.

While people are always moving to New York, others leave. Sometimes they want to escape the problems of life in the big city. In fact, in the 1970s and 1980s, New York's population fell. Now the city is growing again.

Apartment Life

Of course, there are not many houses in Manhattan. Most people live in apartment buildings. Many apartment buildings in the city are called "brownstones" because of the color of the local stone.

Apartments can be very expensive. A lot of people work in the city but have to travel in each day from other areas.

Some of the most expensive apartments are in the beautiful buildings around Central Park.

No Famous People Please!

Many famous people make their home in New York. But sometimes they cannot live where they want. The people in some very expensive apartment buildings can decide who lives in their building. They sometimes refuse famous people because they do not want crowds of reporters outside the doors!

The Brooklyn Bridge

The history of Brooklyn is similar to the story of Manhattan. Farmers first moved to the Brooklyn area in 1636. Like Manhattan, Brooklyn grew and grew. By 1860, 266,000 people lived there. In the next 10 years, 130,000 more people arrived. At that time, the only way between the two cities of Brooklyn and Manhattan was by boat. But in 1866, the New York government decided to build a bridge over the East River. John A. Roebling's plan was the best. He wanted to build a bridge that was "a work of art."

But it was a long, hard job. Around 600 men worked on the bridge. It took 14 years to finish. John A. Roebling did not live to see the completed bridge. In 1869, at the beginning of the job, he hurt his foot badly and he died three weeks later. But Roebling's son Washington continued his father's work. Washington worked hard. He did not just give orders to the bridge workers—he often joined them with tools in his hand.

John Roebling's death was not the last. About 27 bridge workers died. Many of these men were working deep in the waters of the East River. They became sick when they came up too quickly. In 1872, Washington Roebling became sick with the same illness. He did not die, but he was in terrible pain and he could not walk. His wife Emily watched the work on the bridge and reported back to her husband.

At last, in 1883, Manhattan and Brooklyn became one city. The bridge was complete. At the time it was the largest bridge in the world, just over 1 mile (1.8 kilometers) long. It was held up by two big towers that stood in the river. The center part of the bridge was for walkers. The parts on the outside were for horses.

Do you want to buy a bridge?

Many companies helped to pay for the bridge. No one was sure who owned it. Some thieves tried to sell the bridge. A few people believed them and paid!

On May 24, 1883, the bridge opened. Thousands of New Yorkers came to see it. On the first day 150,300 people walked across the bridge and 1,800 vehicles crossed it, too. It cost just 1¢ to walk across that day. But the crowd was too big and some people were pushed off into the water.

The Brooklyn Bridge is still one of the city's greatest sights. New Yorkers love it. In 1984, the city added a bike path. About 150,000 cars and over 2,000 walkers cross the bridge every day. Tourists can walk across to the beautiful neighborhood of Brooklyn Heights. The walk back to Manhattan is even better, with wonderful views of the city.

Getting Around

With so many people in a very small place, how do New Yorkers get around?

The Subway

There are 469 stations with 238 miles (380 kilometers) of subway line in New York City. Most of the trains run under the streets. When the subway first started in 1904, it was only 5¢ for a ride. Now a ticket costs about $2. The trains run all day and night, and around 6 million people use the subway every day.

The subway can be dirty and noisy. But it is also the fastest, cheapest way to get around New York. There is only one problem for tourists—you cannot see the city!

Taxis

New York's bright yellow taxis are a famous sight. There are over 11,000 in the city. New Yorkers sometimes joke that the taxi drivers drive fast and dangerously. In fact, New York taxi drivers must follow a lot of rules. For example, a yellow taxi must take a passenger to any part of the city, even if it is dangerous.

If you get in a taxi in New York, always look for the driver's papers and number. A few taxi drivers do not have these and do not follow the city's rules. A ride in one of these taxis can be expensive or dangerous.

Cars

There are cars everywhere in New York, and the traffic can be terrible. It is not easy to have a car in the city. There are not enough parking spaces. If your car disappears, it was probably not taken by a car thief. It was probably moved by the police. There is a special telephone number that you can call. The police will tell you where your car is.

In fact, many people in New York do not own a car. They can travel by subway or bus. When they buy something big, a truck brings it to their apartment building.

Buses
Over 600 million people use the buses every year in New York City. There are more than 300 bus lines and 4,200 buses. They run on the main streets and usually travel north–south or east–west. Buses can be a great way to see the city, but they are often slow during the busiest times of day for traffic—early morning and late evening. Sometimes it is faster to walk!

Ferries
Ferries take passengers between Manhattan and Brooklyn, Queens, Long Island, and New Jersey. But the most famous ferry travels between Staten Island and Manhattan. The Staten Island Ferry runs 24 hours a day and the ride takes about 25 minutes. Many workers take the ferry to their jobs in Manhattan. But it is great for tourists, too. The ferry gives a wonderful view of the Statue of Liberty. And the price is perfect—the ride is free.

The Staten Island Ferry

Walking
Of course, Manhattan is a small island, so you can always walk. There is a lot to see on the streets. But be careful. More people are hurt by cars in the street than by criminals. Follow the signs on the street corners. They say "Walk" or "Don't walk."

The Green Apple

New Yorkers live in a big city, but they can also enjoy green, open spaces.

Central Park

In the middle of one of the biggest cities in the world, you can have a long, quiet walk under beautiful trees and over green hills. You can take a boat out on a lake or you can sit and watch the wild animals and birds. The place is Central Park. Many New Yorkers cannot imagine the city without the park.

Some tourists think that the park shows natural Manhattan from the days before the city. This is not true. In fact, the park was carefully planned and built. In the 1850s, rich New Yorkers wanted a place like the parks in London and Paris. They wanted a park for walking or riding horses. Frederick Law Olmsted and Calvert Vaux showed their plan for the park in 1858.

But at the time, the land in this area of Manhattan was flat and not very nice. A lot of stone and earth was brought to make the park's hills. Half a million trees and plants were put in the ground. Paths and beautiful stone bridges were built. The lakes and streams under the bridges were not there before. The park was finally finished in 1876.

Today people still walk and ride horses in Central Park. They also ride bikes. Cars can go into the park, but they cannot go everywhere. On the weekend, they cannot go in at all.

Tourists can:

- take a boat on one of the five lakes.
- listen to live music. New Yorkers Simon and Garfunkel sang to a big crowd in Central Park in 1981.
- visit Belvedere Castle. Here they can view the city and the park, and learn about the many animals in the park.
- enjoy the statues. Many of these are for children. There is a statue of Alice at the famous tea party from Lewis Carroll's book *Alice in Wonderland.*
- remember John Lennon in a part of the park called Strawberry Fields. One of the most famous buildings around Central Park is John's old home, the Dakota.

Washington Square Park

A smaller park in the city is important to all Americans. George Washington was made president in Washington Square Park, in Greenwich Village.

The park has been an important part of life in Greenwich Village. When he lived in the area, Bob Dylan sang there. In the 1980s, the park became quite dangerous and many tourists were robbed there. The park is safer now.

Gramercy Park

Gramercy Park is a small, beautiful park. It was built in the 1830s. But not many tourists have seen the park because it is the only private park in the city. Only the people in the expensive buildings around the park can use it.

Coney Island

Brooklyn's Coney Island offers a very different kind of fun. New Yorkers come here to play on the beach and play games.

Tall Stories from the Big City

There are many stories about New York City. Some are true but others are not. Untrue stories are sometimes called "tall stories." Some of New York's stories are as tall as the Empire State Building!

Danger Below the Streets!

The story: Some people say that alligators live under the streets of Manhattan. How did they get there? Children had baby alligators as pets. When the alligators grew, the children threw them away. But they did not die. They lived in the dark under the streets. After years with no sun, the alligators are white. They cannot see, but they can bite . . .

The facts: An alligator *was* found in New York—in East Harlem, in 1935. The animal was near the river. It probably fell off a boat coming from Florida. But scientists say that alligators could not live under the streets for long.

Big Building, Big Stories

There are a lot of stories about the Empire State Building. Which of these stories is true?

1 The building is slowly going down into the ground.
2 Every year there is a race to the top of the building.
3 If you drop a penny from the top of the building, it can kill someone on the street.

Now check your answers:

1 Untrue. The building is built on stone. But like all tall buildings, the top does move from side to side in the wind.
2 True. A good runner can reach the top in about 10 minutes.
3 Untrue. If you drop a penny from the top, it will land on the 86th floor.

Special Days

With people from all over the world, there are lots of special days in New York.

St. Patrick's Day

Many New Yorkers are Irish and St. Patrick's Day on March 17 is an important day for the city. There is a big parade through the center of Manhattan. This is the oldest parade in the city and one of the most famous. If you go to it, remember to wear green, the color of Ireland.

New Year's Eve

On December 31, there is always a big crowd in Times Square. It is one of the biggest parties in the world. Everyone waits for midnight. Then a big, shining glass ball drops as the New Year begins. It reaches the bottom at midnight exactly.

In the rest of the US, people can see the ball at Times Square on television. (But they can't always watch it at midnight—12 o'clock in New York is only 11 o'clock in Chicago or 9 o'clock in Los Angeles.)

Parades

New Yorkers love parades. If one of the city's sports teams is very successful, the city often has a parade. If a famous foreign politician or a king or queen is visiting, there is sometimes a parade. There have been parades for Queen Elizabeth II and Nelson Mandela. There have also been parades for other famous people. In 1969, there was a parade for Neil Armstrong, the first man on the moon. Parades in the city usually start at the south of Manhattan and move north.

The Big, Bad City

A lot of Americans have never been to New York because they are afraid. In their opinion, New York is not just the Big Apple. It is the big, bad city. But how dangerous is New York?

For some years, crime in the city was very bad. In 1969, there were 1,116 murders. After that, there were more than 1,000 murders in the city every year until the 1990s. The 1970s and 1980s were bad years for street crime; a lot of the criminals needed money for drugs. Many people left the city during these years.

Look for the Red Hat

During the bad years of the 1970s, the subway was one of the most dangerous places. Many New Yorkers were afraid to ride the subway because of all the gangs. Curtis Sliwa, a New Yorker from the Bronx, decided to do something. In 1979, he organized a group of people to protect passengers on the subway. At first, there were only 13 in the group. Grateful passengers could see them because they all wore the same T-shirts and red hats. They did not carry guns but they were not afraid to fight. The group grew and took the name "Guardian Angels."

At first, the police did not like the group, but they did not stop them. As more and more people joined, the plan started to work. The Guardian Angels were really helping to make the subway safe. But it was dangerous work. In the first few years, six Guardian Angels were killed as they tried to help people. Now there are groups in many other US cities, too.

Politician Rudy Giuliani was mayor of New York from 1993 until 2001. He promised to "clean up" the city. Under him, the city's police worked hard in areas like Times Square. Before the 1990s, Times Square was full of thieves looking for tourists' wallets and purses. Now the square is a different place. More of the shops are for families. There is even a Disney store there now.

Some people were unhappy with the way that the police cleaned up the city. In the opinion of others, the mayor only tried to make the city better for tourists. But most people in the city think that Giuliani succeeded. New York did become a cleaner and safer place during the 1990s. For 10 years, the number of crimes in New York fell. In 1998, New York was called the safest of all US cities with a population of over one million people. But the fight against crime is never easy. While the number of all crimes in New York has fallen, the number of serious crimes is going up.

Of course, tourists must be careful in a big city. In New York, there are still thieves in subway stations and busy streets. Your time there will be much safer if you follow these suggestions:

- If possible, travel with someone at night.
- Do not go to places where you cannot see other people.
- Do not carry a lot of money with you, and leave jewelry at home or in your hotel.
- Know where you are going.
- If you are afraid, go to a restaurant, hotel, or store.

Shop, Shop, Shop!

If you want to buy something, you can find it in New York. The city has everything, from large department stores to special little shops.

Clothes

75% of all American-made clothes are produced in New York. Shoppers can find every kind of style—from a $1,000 dress in an expensive store to a 1950s T-shirt in a little Greenwich Village shop.

Department Stores

Macy's is the world's biggest department store. It first opened in 1858. The store is now in two buildings in New York. The women's department is on four floors!

The last Thursday of November is Thanksgiving Day in the United States. New Yorkers enjoy the famous Macy's Thanksgiving Day Parade. Americans can watch the parade on television all around the country.

World of Toys

F.A.O. Schwartz is a very big, famous store in New York. The store is full of every kind of toy. In December, you often have to wait in line outside the doors. Tom Hanks danced in the toy store in the 1988 movie *Big*.

Jewelry

Cartier, Gucci, and Tiffany and Co. are all near Central Park. They are beautiful stores selling expensive jewelry. Tiffany's became even more famous after *Breakfast at Tiffany's* (1961). Audrey Hepburn played Holly Golightly in the movie.

* Co.: short for "Company"

Audrey Hepburn as Holly Golightly in Breakfast at Tiffany's

Time to Eat

After a busy day of shopping, most tourists are probably hungry. They are in the right place! There are more than 20,000 restaurants in New York City. You can eat foods from almost every country in the world. The largest restaurant in the city is the Bryant Park Grill. 1,420 people can eat there at the same time!

If you have plenty of money, you can choose from lots of expensive restaurants. Two of the city's famous restaurants are The Tavern on the Green and The Four Seasons. The Tavern on the Green is in Central Park. When it was first built, it was a building for sheep! The Four Seasons is famous for its great food and beautiful rooms. There is even a painting by Picasso on the wall.

Of course, you can always eat cheaply in New York, too. You can buy wonderful sandwiches. And remember—the first hot dog was sold in New York. You don't even need to go inside to eat. You can buy all kinds of food from street sellers.

Out and About

If you like museums, New York is the place for you. The city has almost 100 museums. Here are some of the best:

The Met

New Yorkers usually just call The Metropolitan Museum of Art "the Met." It opened in 1870 with 174 paintings. Now it has over 2 million works of art. There are works by Rembrandt, Van Gogh, and Michaelangelo. The only museum in the world with more Egyptian art is in Cairo.

Museum of Modern Art (MoMA)

This museum has more than 100,000 works of modern art from around the world. There are paintings by famous New York artists like Jackson Pollock and Andy Warhol. Visitors to the museum can also see films and listen to live music.

American Museum of Natural History

This is the largest natural history museum in the world. It has over 32 million things to see.

The Guggenheim Museum

The museum was built by Frank Lloyd Wright in 1959. At first, the museum owners were not happy with the building. In their opinion, some of the walls were too short for the paintings. "Cut the paintings in half!" Wright answered.

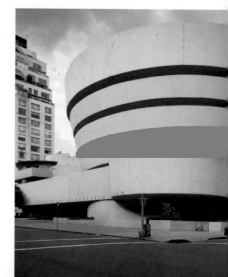

Theater

Most of the city's big theaters are near Times Square and on Broadway. In fact, in the US the name "Broadway" means big theater shows, usually with singing and dancing.

Tickets for popular shows can be very expensive—sometimes hundreds of dollars. There have even been Broadway shows about Broadway. *42nd Street* was about Broadway and New York. It ran for almost 4,000 shows. Mel Brooks' musical *The Producers* is about a terrible Broadway show.

Some New Yorkers think that Broadway shows are mainly for the tourists. But theater-lovers in the city can also see more unusual plays in Greenwich Village and other areas of the city. New Yorkers can see plays and dance and listen to music at the Lincoln Center. Before the center was built, this area of the city was very poor. Leonard Bernstein's famous musical *West Side Story* was about two gangs in this area.

Live Music

Great music is everywhere in the city. You can see famous rock bands in Madison Square Garden. You can hear Mozart at the Lincoln Center and at Carnegie Hall. You can hear all kinds of music in the city's hundreds of clubs. Or you can listen to music in churches, on the streets, and in the subway!

The Way to Carnegie Hall

There is an old New York joke about Carnegie Hall. A tourist is lost and walks up to a New Yorker.

"How can I get to Carnegie Hall?" asks the tourist.

"Practice!" answers the New Yorker.

The Musical City

New York has played a big part in the history of American music. Many great musicians have come from or moved to New York. Jennifer Lopez, Sean Combs (Puff Daddy or P. Diddy), and Billy Joel were all born here. Bob Dylan and Madonna lived in New York. There have been many songs about the city.

Jazz Years

Jazz is probably the most American music, and so of course the greatest American city is very important in its history.

In the 1920s and 1930s, the Cotton Club in Harlem was the best place in town. Great African-American musicians like Duke Ellington played there. But only white people could come to the club to listen.

In later years, New York continued to be the home of the best jazz in the world, with great players like Charlie Parker and Dizzy Gillespie in town.

Duke Ellington—one of America's greatest musicians

A New Sound
In the late 1960s, bands from the West Coast were singing about love and putting flowers in their hair. New York was different. With help from artist Andy Warhol, a new band—The Velvet Underground—started. Their songs were not very happy and they were often about unusual subjects. The rough sound and style of this and other New York bands was very important for later bands like Britain's The Clash and The Sex Pistols.

Party Nights
In the 1970s, everyone was dancing to the dance music called "disco." Studio 54 was the most famous club for this kind of music. For almost ten years, every night in the club was a wild party.

The Birth of Rap
Most people agree that rap music began on the streets of New York in the 1970s. At first, it was only heard in local clubs in the Bronx. The first famous rap song was by a New York group, The Sugarhill Gang. Many other rap artists came from New York—Run DMC, LL Cool J, Chuck D.

Much rap music was about the hard life of the streets. Sometimes the artists did more than sing about it. They lived it. In the late 1990s, there was trouble between rap singers from New York and singers from the West Coast. New York rap star Biggie Smalls was shot dead.

Music Television
New York is also the home of MTV. If you are lucky, you can watch interviews with pop stars in their Manhattan building. When a famous singer visits MTV, the crowds begin to form at around five o'clock in the morning. If that is too early, you can watch the program live in Times Square.

Movie Star City

Most of the film business in the US is on the West Coast, but many movies are made in New York. Every year over 200 are made on the streets of the city. In some of them, the city plays an important part.

- *On the Town* (1949): In this famous musical with Gene Kelly and Frank Sinatra, three men have just 24 hours to play in New York. Then they must return to their ship.
- *Do the Right Thing* (1989): Spike Lee's film looks at the problems as a neighborhood changes. The movie was made in Brooklyn. Lee wanted the movie to look at real problems in the city.
- *When Harry Met Sally* (1989): They live in the city. We see them walking in Central Park.
- *Ghostbusters* (1984): They live in an old fire station in TriBeCa. The building at the end of the movie is west of Central Park.
- *Spiderman* (2001): Spiderman travels all around the city. In one part of the movie, he climbs on the Queensboro Bridge.

Spiderman on the Queensboro Bridge

New York City is probably most important to two very different movie-makers—Martin Scorsese and Woody Allen.

Scorsese and actor Robert DeNiro grew up in Little Italy. Scorsese's early movie *Mean Streets* (1973) was about street life in their old neighborhood. Many of Scorsese's other movies also look at the dark side of life in New York. In *Taxi Driver* (1976), Travis Bickle (Robert DeNiro) is the taxi driver. Watching the city's street life, he says, "All the animals come out at night." In 2002, Scorsese turned to the city's older history with *The Gangs of New York*. The movie starred Leonardo DiCaprio.

Woody Allen grew up in Brooklyn but lives now in one of the expensive buildings near Central Park. He has made most of his movies in the city. His 1979 black-and-white movie *Manhattan* is named after the island. It uses famous music that George Gershwin wrote about New York. The movie is like a love letter to Allen's home city. Other New York movies by Allen are *Annie Hall* (1977) and *Hannah and Her Sisters* (1986).

Back to New York

For some years, it was quite expensive to film in New York. Some movie-makers even filmed New York stories in other big cities, like Toronto. But now they are returning to the Big Apple. The city's mayor loves movie-makers to come to New York. Movies bring jobs to the city. Then, later, they help to bring more and more tourists.

Television

In the early days of television, all of the big American television companies were in New York. During the 1950s, many of these programs were watched by the country as they were made. Now most TV programs in the US are made in Los Angeles. But the main companies' daily news programs and some talk shows are made in New York.

Some programs in New York are still made in front of a real crowd. If you want to go, you can write to the television company for a free ticket. One of the country's favorite shows, *Saturday Night Live*, always begins with the words, "Live from New York … it's Saturday night!"

Rockefeller Center

Rockefeller Center is a group of 19 buildings in the middle of Manhattan. They were all owned by one of the richest men in the world, John D. Rockefeller, Jr.* The center has many works of art.

In the 1950s, television companies and radio stations started at the Rockefeller Center. Today it is the home of NBC, one of the country's biggest television companies. Every morning, there is a crowd of people outside the center. They all want to be on NBC's morning news program.

* Jr.: the son of a man with the same name

"I'll be there for you!"

The NBC program *Friends* was one of the biggest TV successes in the world. The show was about six good friends living in Manhattan. Some New Yorkers probably wanted to know how they paid for their big apartments!

The program was about New York, but it was not made there. Almost all of the show was made in California. But two of the actors have lived in New York in real life.

- Jennifer Aniston (Rachel Green in the show) grew up in the city. When she was 11, one of her paintings was shown at the Met. She started acting in "off Broadway" theater.

- David Schwimmer (Ross Geller in the show) was born in New York. But, like the show *Friends*, the actor moved to Los Angeles.

Friends is one of the most popular television programs in the world.

Sports in the City

Like most Americans, New Yorkers love sports, and the city is home to many sports teams. You can see the most popular teams at these places:

Football
Both of New York's teams, the Jets and the Giants, play in the same stadium in New Jersey.

Baseball
The New York Yankees play at Yankee Stadium in the Bronx. The New York Mets are at Shea Stadium in Queens.

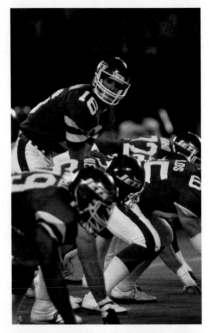

The New York Jets

Basketball
The New York Knicks play at Madison Square Garden. You can also see the Harlem Globetrotters there—and other sports, too.

The New York Knicks

If you like tennis, you can go to the US Tennis Center in Queens. But if you want to go to a big game, you need to buy your ticket three months before the day.

Of course, New Yorkers do not just *watch* sports. Many of them love to get outside and play. In the morning, before work, you can see lots of runners in Central Park.

Basketball is one of the most popular sports in the city. Players do not need a big field or a lot of people to have a game.

The Hard Way to See New York!

On a Sunday in November every year, New Yorkers come out to watch people run through the city. In the first year, 127 people ran all around Central Park. Now there are more than 22,000 runners, and the race takes them around all five areas of the city. The 26.2 mile (42 kilometer) race starts at the Verrazano Bridge and ends at Tavern on the Green in Central Park.

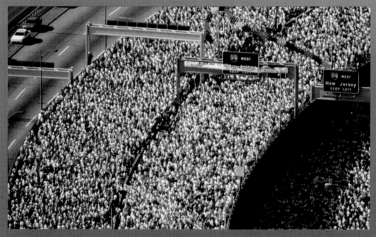

Racing around the city

The Capital of the World?

New York is not the capital of the United States. For many New Yorkers, it is more than that—it is the capital of the world!

The United Nations

The United Nations building is in New York. The world organization began in 1945 and 189 countries now belong. The building looks over the East River, on the east side of Manhattan. In fact, this building is not part of the United States. It is international. It even has its own stamps.

The United Nations building

Wall Street

New York is one of the business centers of the world, and Wall Street is the heart of the city's financial area. It is in the south of the island—in lower Manhattan. Visitors can take a tour of the area and see the money capital at work. Millions of dollars are made and lost there.

People on Wall Street work hard and make a lot of money, but some of them play even harder. A few think that they own the world. Oliver Stone's 1987 movie *Wall Street*, with Michael Douglas, looked at these people. The film was not always kind to them.

The map below shows some of the sights on the small island of Manhattan that you have read about:

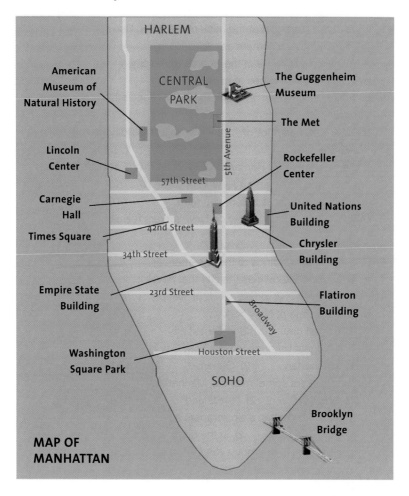

HARLEM

American Museum of Natural History

CENTRAL PARK

The Guggenheim Museum

The Met

5th Avenue

Lincoln Center

Rockefeller Center

57th Street

Carnegie Hall

United Nations Building

42nd Street

Times Square

Chrysler Building

34th Street

Empire State Building

23rd Street

Flatiron Building

Broadway

Washington Square Park

Houston Street

SOHO

Brooklyn Bridge

MAP OF MANHATTAN

So that is New York. It is big and crowded. It can be noisy and dirty. It is also a wonderful place. Is it the most exciting city on earth? Probably. And if you do not agree, do not tell a New Yorker!

ACTIVITIES

Pages 1–7

Before you read

1 Look at the Word List at the back of the book. Use some of the words to complete these sentences.
  a All of the banks are in the … area of the city.
  b I bought these shoes at my favorite … .
  c Many … arrive in the United States from other countries every year.
  d New York has a lot of …, but the tallest building in the world is in another city.
  e There are a lot of Roman and Egyptian things at the … .

2 What do you know about New York City? What do you want to learn about it? Make notes before you read.

3 Read the Introduction. How do New Yorkers feel about their city?

While you read

4 Circle the right endings to these sentences.
  a New York is known as the city that never … .
    1) eats   **2)** drives   **3)** sleeps
  b It is the state of New York's … .
    1) largest city   **2)** greenest city   **3)** capital
  c The biggest borough in New York City is … .
    1) Manhattan   **2)** Queens   **3)** Brooklyn
  d New Yorkers sometimes call Manhattan … .
    1) "the City"   **2)** "the Island"   **3)** "the Neighborhood"
  e Most of Manhattan's skyscrapers are … .
    1) in the south   **2)** in the north   **3)** in the central area
  f The building in the movie *King Kong* is … .
    1) the Empire State Building   **3)** the Chrysler Building
    2) the Flatiron Building
  g The Chrysler Building was built to look like … .
    1) a church   **2)** a car wheel   **3)** a train

h Rudy Giuliani was ... .

    1) the mayor of the city   **3)** an actor

    2) the builder of the World Trade Center

After you read

5 Answer these questions.

  a How can you reach Manhattan from the other boroughs?

  b Why has the city introduced new rules for skyscrapers?

  c In March–April, 2002 how did the city remember the people who died on September 11, 2001?

6 You have one afternoon in New York. Discuss which building you want to visit, and why.

Pages 8–17

Before you read

7 Answer these questions, and then read. Were you right?

  a Who were the first people on the island of Manhattan?

  b Which country gave the Statue of Liberty to the United States?

  c Why was Ellis Island important to many new Americans?

  d How many New Yorkers were born in a different country?

While you read

8 Are these sentences right (✓) or wrong (✗)?

  a The first European on Manhattan was British.   .....

  b The city's first name was New Amsterdam.   .....

  c New York was the country's capital for a short time.   .....

  d Tourists can climb up to the Statue of Liberty's hand.   .....

  e Liberty Island was called Bedloe's Island.   .....

  f All new immigrants on boats went to Ellis Island.   .....

  g There is a museum on Ellis Island now.   .....

  h More Italians live in Rome than in New York.   .....

  i The population of New York is falling.   .....

After you read

9 Read the sentences. What does each sentence describe?

  a It was called Manna Hatta.

  b It arrived in 220 boxes.

    c This was the gateway to a new country for millions of immigrants.

    d This area got its name because it is south of Houston Street.

    e Many African-Americans lived in this area, north of Central Park.

10 Some people have called New York "a city of immigrants." Do you agree? Has this made New York different from most places? How?

Pages 18–24

Before you read

11 Match the sentences with the chapter titles, below.

    a Some people say that alligators live under the streets of Manhattan.

    b It is not easy to have a car in the city.

    c You can take a boat out on a lake or you can sit and watch the wild animals and birds.

    d It was held up by two big towers that stood in the river.

       "The Brooklyn Bridge"   "Getting Around"

       "The Green Apple"   "Tall Stories from the Big City"

While you read

12 Complete the sentences.

    a The Brooklyn Bridge joins Brooklyn and ....

    b It took .... years to finish the bridge.

    c There are more than .... taxis in the city, and .... buses.

    d The most famous ferry travels between Manhattan and ....

    e There are .... lakes in Central Park.

    f In 1935, an .... was found in East Harlem.

    g Every year there is a .... to the top of the Empire State Building.

After you read

13 Discuss these questions.

    a In what different ways can people cross the Brooklyn Bridge today?

    b Why do some tourists not want to take the subway in the city?

    c Why is Central Park not "natural?"

14 Think of a new "tall story" about a different animal in New York City.

15 Look back at the pictures on pages 1–24. Discuss what you have learned about the places in the pictures.

Pages 25–31

Before you read

16 Do you think that New York is a dangerous city? Why (not)?

17 Discuss how much you enjoy these. Give them numbers from 5 (very enjoyable) down to 0.

parades   shopping   restaurants   museums   theater   live music

While you read

18 Answer these questions.

   a What is the city's oldest parade? ....

   b Who was there a parade for in 1969? ....

   c What group helps to make the subway safe? ....

   d What shop is in the 1988 movie *Big*? ....

   e In which restaurant is there a painting by
      Picasso? ....

   f Which museum building were the owners
      unhappy with at first? ....

   g Which musical is about a Broadway show? ....

   h Where can New Yorkers see more unusual
      plays? ....

After you read

19 Which of these statements are untrue? Correct them.

   a Many New Yorkers go to Times Square on New Year's Eve.

   b The "Guardian Angels" are a group of criminals.

   c Macy's is the biggest department store in New York.

   d The Met has more Egyptian art than any other museum in the world.

   e The Four Seasons restaurant is in Central Park.

   f Tourists can see musical theater shows "on Broadway."

20 A friend is traveling to New York on business and is afraid. What can you suggest to make the trip safe?

Pages 32–41

Before you read

21 Discuss these questions.

   a What kind of music do you think of when you think of New York City?

   b What movies have you seen about New York? Discuss one. What does the movie tell you about life in the city? Do you think that it is a true picture?

While you read

22 Circle the correct answer.

   a Who was born in New York City?

   Madonna   Jennifer Lopez

   b Which kind of music began on the streets of New York?

   jazz   rap music

   c Which borough was *Do The Right Thing* filmed in?

   Brooklyn   The Bronx

   d Who made a film about a taxi driver in the city?

   Woody Allen   Martin Scorsese

   e What television company is at Rockefeller Center?

   NBC   MTV

   f Where was most of *Friends* made?

   New York City   California

   g What sport do the New York Mets play?

   baseball   basketball

   h Where can you watch international tennis?

   Staten Island   Queens

   i When did the United Nations begin?

   1945   1989

   j What country is the United Nations building part of?

   no country   the United States

After you read

23 Discuss these questions. Explain your answers.

   a Which of the kinds of music on pages 32–33 do you like most?

   b Which of the movies on pages 34–35 would you like to see (again)?

   c Which of the sports on pages 38–39 would you most like to watch in New York?

24 Do you agree that New York is "the capital of the world?" Why (not)?

25 Look again at your notes for question 2. Have you learned the answers to all your questions? What do you still want to know about the city?

Writing

26 You are going to New York. Make a list of ten things that you want to do there. Explain why.

27 You are on vacation in New York. Write a postcard to a friend at home.

28 A New York magazine wants to know what people in other countries think about the city's people and buildings. Give your opinions or the opinions of someone you know.

29 You are preparing a page for the Internet to sell vacations in New York. You want to say that it is "the most exciting city in the world." What will the page say and show? Make notes.

30 You are making a movie about a new immigrant in New York. Write some ideas for the story.

31 You are a teacher. Explain to your students, on paper, some of the history of New York City. Use words and pictures.

32 How is the biggest city in your country different from New York? How is it similar? Compare the two.

33 Choose a city in your country. Write a short guide for foreign tourists. What should they see and do?

WORD LIST

alligator (n) a large, long animal that lives in and near water in the United States and China. Alligators kill and eat smaller animals, and sometimes people.

baseball (n) a game of two teams. You hit the ball and run. If you are successful, you win points.

basketball (n) a game of two teams. You run, throw the ball, and try to win points.

crown (n) something round that kings and queens wear on their heads

department store (n) a large store that sells many different products

ferry (n) a boat that carries people, and often cars, across a narrow area of water

financial (adj) about money

immigrant (n) someone who moves into a country from another country

jazz (n) a type of music that was first played around a hundred years ago by Black Americans

jewelry (n) pretty things that you wear on your hands, around your neck, or on your clothes

liberty (n) the state of being free

mayor (n) the most important person in the government of a town or city

museum (n) a building where visitors can see important things from—for example—history or science

parade (n) an activity on a special day in which people and vehicles move slowly through the streets to the sound of music

rap music (n) a kind of music that began in American cities in the early 1970s. Rappers speak while music plays behind their words.

sight (n) a famous and interesting place; something that you can see

skyscraper (n) a very tall building in a city, usually at least 100 meters tall

stadium (n) a large area for playing sports, with a building and seats around it

statue (n) something that looks like a person or an animal. Statues are usually made of stone or metal.

tower (n) a tall, narrow building, or part of a building

Billy Elliot
Melvin Burgess

Eleven-year-old Billy Elliot is different from other boys. He is not very clever or good at sport. Then, one day, he discovers ballet dancing. Finally he has found something that he can do well. But everybody knows that ballet is for girls, not boys! Will Billy continue to dance? Or have his father and brother got other plans for him?

Forrest Gump
Winston Groom

Everybody tells Forrest Gump that he's an idiot. But he's a great football player, and he plays the harmonica beautifully. He's also a brave soldier. But can he ever marry the girl he loves? This story of his journey through life is sometimes sad and sometimes very funny.

Matilda
Roald Dahl

Matilda is a clever and unusual little girl. But her parents aren't interested in her, and the terrible head teacher at her school hates clever children. But Matilda finds a way to be strong, and the results are very funny.

There are hundreds of Penguin Readers to choose from – world classics, film adaptations, modern-day crime and adventure, short stories, biographies, American classics, non-fiction, plays ...

For a complete list of all Penguin Readers titles, please contact your local Pearson Longman office or visit our website.

www.penguinreaders.com

Jim Smiley and his Jumping Frog and Other Stories
Mark Twain

Mark Twain is one of America's most famous and best-loved writers. He wrote about every important subject of his time. Twain's stories are usually amusing but with a serious message too. You will read about people's hopes and fears, happiness and terrible sadness – and wonderful practical jokes!

Rain Man
Leonore Fleischer

Charlie Babbit needs money. But when his rich father dies, Charlie gets two surprises. One: he has a brother, Raymond, who lives in a special hospital. Two: all their father's money goes to Raymond. Charlie is angry, but the journey across America with Raymond changes his life.

The Thirty-nine Steps
John Buchan

A man is killed in Richard Hannay's home. Before his death he tells Hannay a dangerous secret. Now Hannay's life is in danger. Who are his enemies and what are they trying to do? And how will he solve the mystery of 'the thirty-nine steps'?

There are hundreds of Penguin Readers to choose from – world classics, film adaptations, modern-day crime and adventure, short stories, biographies, American classics, non-fiction, plays ...

For a complete list of all Penguin Readers titles, please contact your local Pearson Longman office or visit our website.

Braveheart
Randall Wallace

'Sons of Scotland, you have come here to fight as free men . . . if you fight perhaps you'll die.'

Braveheart is the true story of William Wallace who led his people to fight for the country they loved.

Braveheart is an exhilarating and moving film directed by and starring Mel Gibson. It won five Oscars at the Academy Awards.

The No. 1 Ladies' Detective Agency
Alexander McCall Smith

Precious Ramotswe is a kind, warm hearted and large African lady. She is also the only female private detective in Botswana. Her agency – the No. 1 Ladies' Detective Agency – is the best in the country. With the help of her secretary, Mma Makutsi, and her best friend, Mr JLB Matekoni, she solves a number of difficult – and sometimes dangerous – problems. A missing husband, a missing finger and a missing child – she will solve these mysteries in her own special way.

The Island of Dr Moreau
H. G. Wells

Edward Prendick is travelling in the South Pacific when his ship goes down. He is saved after many days at sea by another ship, and a passenger, Montgomery, nurses him back to health. Prendick becomes interested in the mystery of Montgomery's life. Why does he live on an unknown Pacific island? Why is he taking animals there? And should Prendick fear the dark secrets of Montgomery's master – the even more mysterious Doctor Moreau?

There are hundreds of Penguin Readers to choose from – world classics, film adaptations, modern-day crime and adventure, short stories, biographies, American classics, non-fiction, plays ...

For a complete list of all Penguin Readers titles, please contact your local Pearson Longman office or visit our website.

www.penguinreaders.com

Longman Dictionaries

Express yourself with confidence!

*Longman has led the way in ELT dictionaries since 1935.
We constantly talk to students and teachers around the
world to find out what they need from a learner's dictionary.*

Why choose a Longman dictionary?

Easy to understand

Longman invented the Defining Vocabulary – 2000 of the most
common words which are used to write the definitions in our
dictionaries. So Longman definitions are always clear and easy
to understand.

Real, natural English

All Longman dictionaries contain natural examples taken from
real-life that help explain the meaning of a word and show you
how to use it in context.

Avoid common mistakes

Longman dictionaries are written specially for learners, and we
make sure that you get all the help you need to avoid common
mistakes. We analyse typical learners' mistakes and include
notes on how to avoid them.

Innovative CD-ROMs

Longman are leaders in dictionary CD-ROM innovation. Did
you know that a dictionary CD-ROM includes features to help
improve your pronunciation, help you practice for exams and
improve your writing skills?

**For details of all Longman dictionaries, and to choose
the one that's right for you, visit our website:**

www.longman.com/dictionaries